Jess has a job to do.
She gets a pan.
"Come and get it, Red Hen!"

1

Red Hen gets her food.
Then Jess gets an egg from Red Hen.

 2

Jess runs to the bin.
"Come and get it, Bonnie!"

Bonnie gets her food.
Then Jess gets milk from Bonnie.

 4

Jess nods to Sunnie.
"Come and get it, Sunnie!"

5

Sunnie gets his food.
Then Sunnie digs up yams for Jess.

 6

Mom says, "Come and get it, Jess!"
Jess runs into the house.

Jess gets eggs and milk and yams.
Yum! Yum! Yum!

 8